Date: 4/10/15

J 736.982 OWE
Owen, Ruth,
Mountain animals /

ORIGAMI SAFARI

Mountain Animals

By Ruth Owen

WINDMILL
BOOKS™

New York

Published in 2015 by Windmill Books, An Imprint of Rosen Publishing
29 East 21st Street, New York, NY 10010

First Edition

Produced for Rosen by Ruby Tuesday Books Ltd
Editor for Ruby Tuesday Books Ltd: Mark J. Sachner
Designer: Emma Randall

Photo Credits:
Cover, 1, 3, 5, 6–7, 8–9, 10–11, 12–13, 14–15, 16–17, 18–19, 20–21, 22–23,
24–25, 26–27, 28–29, 31 © Ruby Tuesday Books; cover, 4–5, 6, 10,
14, 18, 22, 26 © Shutterstock.

Library of Congress Cataloging-in-Publication Data

Owen, Ruth, 1967– author.
 Mountain animals / by Ruth Owen. — First Edition.
     pages cm. — (Origami safari)
 Includes index.
 ISBN 978-1-4777-9257-5 (library binding) —
 ISBN 978-1-4777-9258-2 (pbk.) — ISBN 978-1-4777-9259-9 (6-pack)
 1. Origami—Juvenile literature. 2. Mountain animals—Juvenile
literature. 3. Forest animals in art—Juvenile literature. 4. Animals in
art—Juvenile literature. I. Title.
 TT872.5.O936 2015
 736.982— dc23
                                                    2014014030

Manufactured in the United States of America

CPSIA Compliance Information: Batch #WS14WM: For Further Information contact Rosen Publishing, New York, New York at 1-866-478-0556

Contents

Mountain Origami

Around the world, many animals make their homes on the slopes of rocky mountains. Mountain **habitats** can be very cold and snowy or cool and rainy.

On the slopes of some mountains, there are forests of **coniferous** trees. Other mountains are home to **rain forests** or forests of **bamboo**.

Many different animals live on mountains and in forests. In this book you will get to meet six of these fascinating wild animals, and you will also get the chance to make a fantastic **origami** model of each one. All you need is some paper, and you will be ready to follow the step-by-step instructions to make your own collection of origami animals.

A mountain habitat

Origami Mountain Goat

Mountain goats live on the rocky slopes of mountains in the United States, including the Rocky Mountains.

These goats have hooves made up of two toes that spread wide apart to help the animals balance. They also have rough pads on the soles of their feet to help their feet grip icy, slippery rocks. To protect them from cold winds, they have long, thick coats of hair.

Mountain goats move around easily on ledges at terrifying heights and can jump up to 12 feet (3.7 m) in a single leap!

YOU WILL NEED:

- To make a mountain goat, one sheet of white paper
- Scissors

Step 1:

Fold the paper in half diagonally, crease, and then unfold.

Fold the top point and the bottom point into the center crease to create a kite shape, and crease.

Step 2:

Now fold points A and B into the center crease, and crease well.

A

B

A
B

B

Step 3:

Take hold of point A and open up the fold to create a pocket. Then gently squash the pocket down to create a new point.

Pocket

New point

Repeat on the other side with point B.

Step 4:

Turn the model over. Fold point D up to meet point C, and crease well.

Neck

Step 5:

To make the goat's neck, fold up the left-hand side of the model, crease well, and then unfold.

Reverse folded neck

Now open out the neck section, and using the creases you've just made, reverse fold the neck section so it tucks back on itself inside the body.

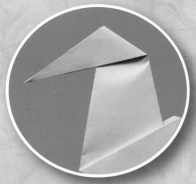

Step 6:

To make the goat's head, fold down the top of the neck, crease well, and unfold.

Reverse folded head

Cut along the dotted line

Now open out the head section and reverse fold it so that the head section tucks in on itself inside the top of the neck.

Now cut along the top ridge on each side of the head to make a sliver of paper. Fold up the two slivers to create the goat's horns.

Fold down the tip of the head to give the goat a blunt nose and to create its beard. Cut off the tip of the beard as shown.

Horns

Fold up the slivers of paper to make horns.

Beard

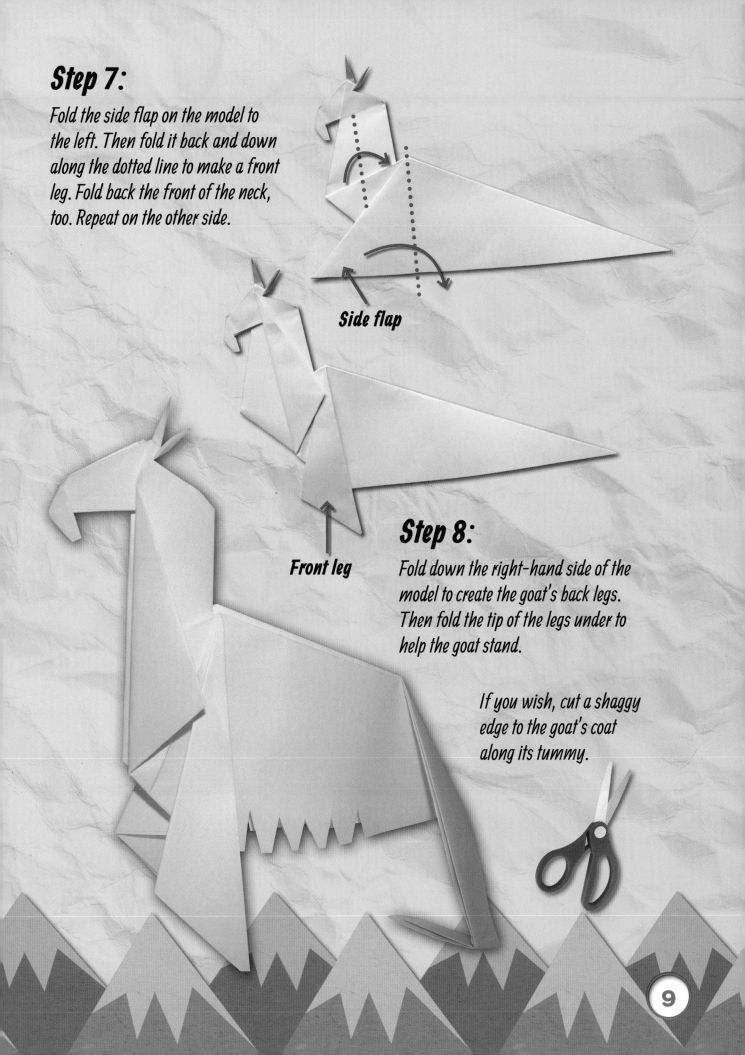

Step 7:

Fold the side flap on the model to the left. Then fold it back and down along the dotted line to make a front leg. Fold back the front of the neck, too. Repeat on the other side.

Side flap

Front leg

Step 8:

Fold down the right-hand side of the model to create the goat's back legs. Then fold the tip of the legs under to help the goat stand.

If you wish, cut a shaggy edge to the goat's coat along its tummy.

Origami Mountain Lion

Mountain lions are also called pumas, panthers, and cougars. They live in mountainous forests and grasslands of North, Central, and South America. These powerful **predators** can leap 20 feet (6 m) up a mountainside. That's like jumping onto the roof of a two-story building!

Mountain lions hunt many kinds of **prey**, including deer, wild pigs, raccoons, and skunks. They will even catch and eat creatures as small as insects.

Female mountain lions give birth to their cubs in a den tucked away in a cave or thick bushes. When the cubs are between 6 and 12 months old, they leave the safety of their den and go off to hunt on their own.

YOU WILL NEED:

- To make a mountain lion, a sheet of orange or brown paper
- Scissors
- A marker

Step 1:

Fold the paper in half, crease, and then unfold.

Fold the sides into the center crease to create a kite shape, and crease.

Step 2:

Turn the model over. Fold up the bottom point of the model to meet the top point, and crease.

Step 3:

Now fold the point back down again along the dotted line so that edge A is level with edge B. Crease well.

Edge A

Edge B

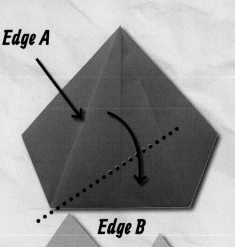

Step 4:

Pick up your model. Fold section D behind section C. At the same time, fold section E down and behind section F.

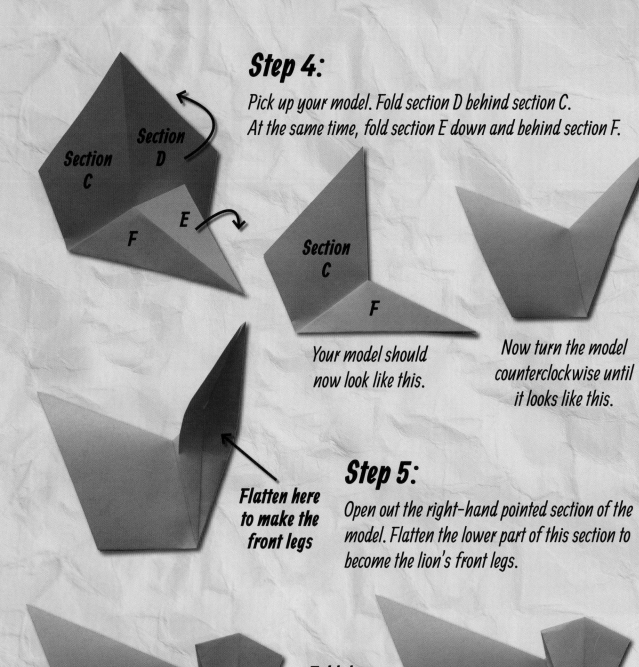

Section C
Section D
F
E

Section C
F

Your model should now look like this.

Now turn the model counterclockwise until it looks like this.

Flatten here to make the front legs

Step 5:

Open out the right-hand pointed section of the model. Flatten the lower part of this section to become the lion's front legs.

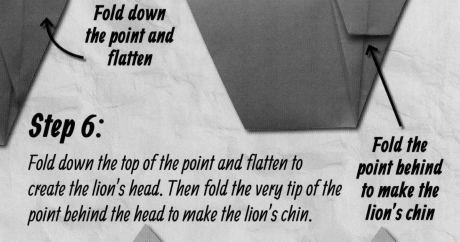

Fold down the point and flatten

Fold the point behind to make the lion's chin

Step 6:

Fold down the top of the point and flatten to create the lion's head. Then fold the very tip of the point behind the head to make the lion's chin.

Step 7:

To make the lion a long tail, cut along the left-hand edge of the model following the dotted line. Then fold over the left-hand point of the model, crease, and unfold.

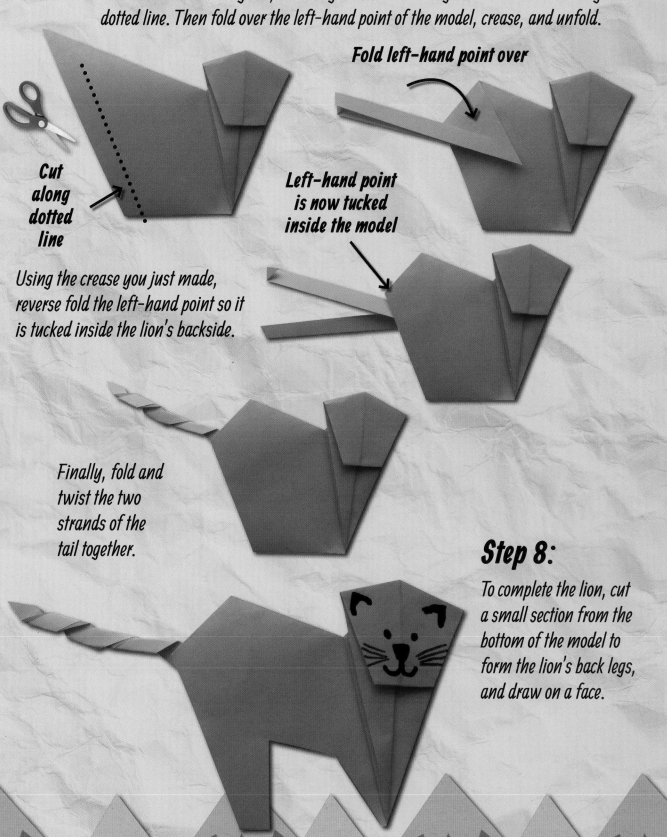

Fold left-hand point over

Cut along dotted line

Left-hand point is now tucked inside the model

Using the crease you just made, reverse fold the left-hand point so it is tucked inside the lion's backside.

Finally, fold and twist the two strands of the tail together.

Step 8:

To complete the lion, cut a small section from the bottom of the model to form the lion's back legs, and draw on a face.

Origami Condor

The Andes Mountains in South America are home to the Andean condor. These huge black birds can often be seen soaring high above the rocky slopes of mountains.

An adult Andean condor's body is about 4 feet (1.2 m) long. Its wings, when fully open in flight, can measure 10 feet (3 m) from wing tip to wing tip.

Condors are **scavengers**, which means they feed on the dead bodies of other animals. They use their good eyesight to spot meals from high above the ground. Feeding on dead **carcasses** sounds disgusting, but these birds help keep the **environment** in which they live clean and healthy by cleaning up waste matter.

YOU WILL NEED:

- To make a condor, a sheet of paper that's black on one side
- Scissors

Step 1:

Place the paper black side down, fold in half diagonally, and crease.

Step 2:

Now take the bottom point of the triangle you've made and fold it upward to create a new smaller triangle. Crease well.

Step 3:

Fold the top layer of paper from the small triangle back down so that you create a pleat, and crease.

Pleat

Step 4:

Now turn the model 90 degrees counterclockwise. Fold the top half of the model down along the dotted line, and crease well.

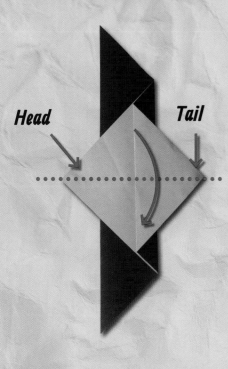

Head **Tail**

Step 5:

Next, fold up the condor's top wing along the dotted line, and crease well.

Turn your model over and repeat on the other wing. Your model should now look like this.

Underside of wing

Tail

Head

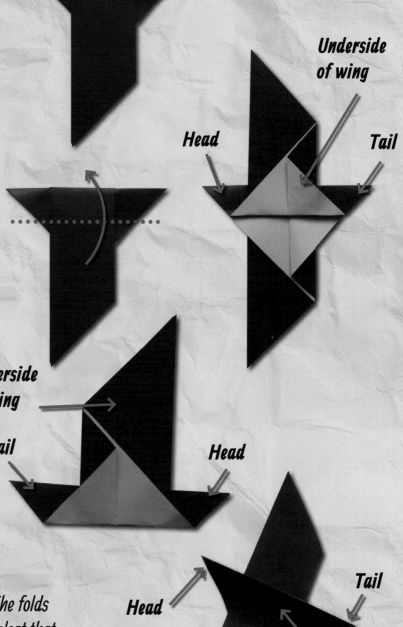

Underside of wing

Head **Tail**

Underside of wing

Tail **Head**

Step 6:

Now fold the wings back down. The folds you made in step 5 have made a pleat that has created a body for the condor.

Head **Tail**

Body

Step 7:

To complete the condor's head, take hold of the head point and fold and twist it down.

Head

Step 8:

Cut feathers into the tips of the condor's wings.

Step 9:

Squash down the tail section.

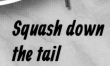

Squash down the tail

Then cut feathers into the condor's tail, and your model is complete.

Origami Wolf

Wolves live in **wilderness** areas where there are thick forests and mountains.

These wild members of the dog family live in family groups called packs. The leaders of the pack are the alpha male and alpha female. They are the oldest, strongest members of the group. The other members of the pack are usually the alpha pair's young cubs and grown-up cubs from previous years.

A wolf pack will have a **territory**. This is the area where the family lives and hunts for food. The pack works as a team, hunting large prey such as deer, moose, bison, and mountain goats.

- To make a wolf, a sheet of gray, brown, orange, white, or black paper
- A marker

Step 1:

Place the paper colored side down. Fold in half along the dotted line, and crease.

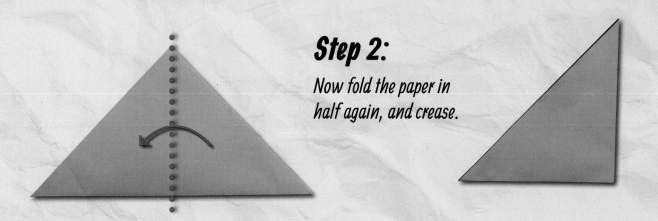

Step 2:

Now fold the paper in half again, and crease.

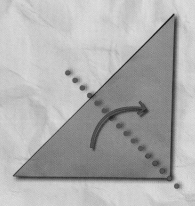

Step 3:

Next fold up the bottom half of the model, and crease. You should only be folding the top layer of paper at this stage.

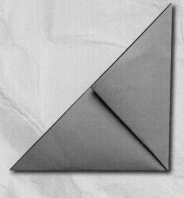

Step 4:

Turn the model over. Fold up the bottom half of the model along the dotted line, and crease.

Step 5:

Turn the model clockwise.

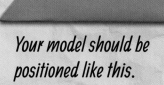

Your model should be positioned like this.

Step 6:

Fold the right-hand side of the model along the dotted line into the center of the model. Crease hard. Fold the left-hand point of the model along the dotted line into the center, and crease hard.

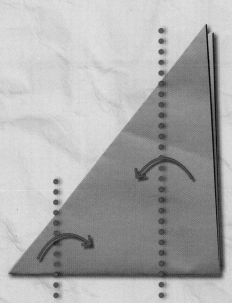

Step 7:

Now open out the fold you've just made on the right-hand side of the model. Form the wolf's ears from the two outside points. Fold down and flatten the middle section to create the wolf's face.

Ear

Face

Ear

Tail

Front Leg

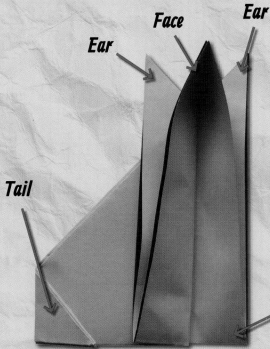

Finally, use the marker to give your wolf a black nose and eyes.

Origami Mountain Gorilla

Mountain gorillas live in cold, wet, misty rain forests on mountains and volcanoes in Africa.

They live in small family groups. A group usually has an adult male, three or four adult females and their babies, and several young gorillas. The family is led by the male, who is known as a silverback because of the silver-colored hair on his back. The silverback is the father of most of the babies in the group.

Mountain gorillas spend about half of each day peacefully munching plants. They eat nettles, thistles, celery, flowers, bark, roots, and berries. A favorite food is bamboo. At night, each adult gorilla makes a sleeping nest of leaves and branches in a tree or on the ground.

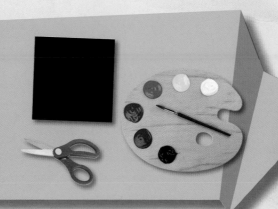

- To make a gorilla, one sheet of black paper
- Paints and a paintbrush
- Scissors

Step 1:

Place the paper black side down, fold in half along the dotted line, crease, and then unfold. Then fold each half into the center crease to create a kite shape, and crease.

Step 2:

Now fold the model in half.

Step 3:

Fold over the left-hand edge of the model along the dotted line, and crease well.

Step 4:

To shape the gorilla's back legs and backside, fold in the bottom right-hand point of the model, crease well, and then unfold. Then using the creases you've just made, reverse fold this section so it's tucked inside the body.

Reverse fold

Step 5:

Now open out the fold you made on the left-hand side of the model to create a hood-like pocket. Flatten the bottom of this section against the gorilla's body to form its front legs.

Open out to form a hood-like pocket.

Flatten to make the gorilla's front legs.

Ridge on head

Step 6:

Squash down and flatten the top section of the pocket. You want to make sure that your gorilla's head has a ridge or point at the top.

Step 7:

To shape the gorilla's head fold behind the two side points and the bottom point, and crease well.

Cut along dotted line

Then cut out a small section from the bottom of the model to complete the gorilla's legs.

Step 8:

To make the gorilla's mouth, fold up the bottom of the face, crease, and then fold back down, making a small pleat. If you wish, you can paint a face onto your gorilla.

Origami Giant Panda

Giant pandas live in cold, mountainous bamboo and coniferous forests in China.

They eat a variety of grasses and other plants, as well as insects and even the rotting bodies of other animals. Their favorite food is bamboo, and their strong jawbones and cheek muscles help them crush and chew tough bamboo stalks and leaves. Because bamboo doesn't contain very many **nutrients**, giant pandas spend up to 12 hours eating about 84 pounds (38 kg) of bamboo every day.

Adult giant pandas weigh between 176 and 330 pounds (80 to 150 kg). Their babies are quite small, however. Panda cubs start off no larger than a stick of butter!

Step 1:

Place the paper black side down. Fold in half along the dotted lines, crease, and then unfold.

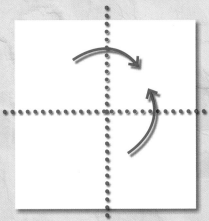

Step 2:

Turn the paper over. Now fold the paper in half diagonally along the dotted lines, crease, and unfold.

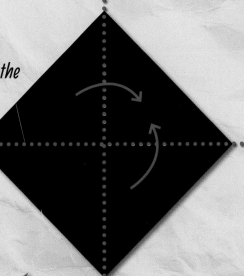

Squash in here

Squash in here

Squash in here

This triangle should end up on top of the model.

Step 3:

Turn the paper over again and it should now look like this.

Using the creases you made in steps 1 and 2, squash the model together to create a triangle shape.

Your model should look like this.

Step 4:

Fold up the two side points of the model. Only fold the top layer of paper.

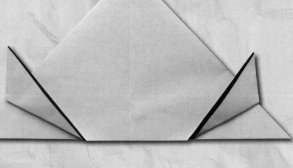

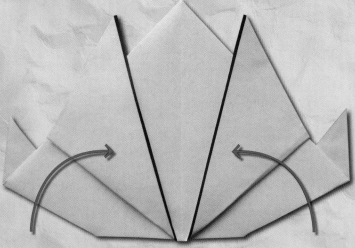

Step 5:

Turn the model over. Now fold up the two side points, again, only folding the top layer of paper.

Step 6:

Open out all the folds you've made. Your paper should look like this.

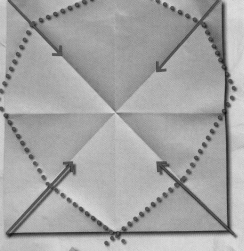

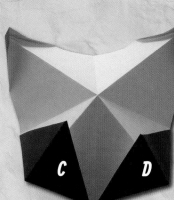

A   B

Now lift up your paper and fold each of the four corners back on itself along the dotted lines. Your model will look just as it did in step 3 but will now have a black section enclosing each corner.

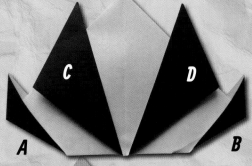

C   D

A   B

Now gently squash the model, exactly as you did in step 3, so that it flattens and looks like this.

Step 7:

Fold the right side of the model behind the left side along the center crease. Then turn the model 90 degrees counterclockwise.

Head →   **Front leg**   ← **Back leg**

You can now see the panda shape emerging.

Step 8:

Fold behind

Fold the side point of the panda's front leg behind. Repeat on the other side.

Fold behind

Fold the top edge of the model back along the dotted line, crease hard, and then unfold.

Reverse fold the panda's back.

Now use the crease you've just made to make a reverse fold tucked into the panda's back.

Use a marker to draw on black ears and eye patches. Your giant panda is complete!

Step 9:

Finally, fold the tip of the panda's head behind, and crease. Then fold it forward again, making a small pleat.

Glossary

bamboo (bam-BOO)
A thick-stemmed type of grass. Bamboos often grow very fast.

carcasses (CAR-kus-ez) Dead bodies. This word is usually used to describe the dead bodies of animals.

coniferous (kah-NIH-fur-us)
Referring to trees that often grow in cold, tough habitats and do not lose their leaves in winter. Many have needlelike leaves.

environment (en-VY-ern-ment)
The area where plants and animals live, along with all the things, such as weather, that affect the area.

habitats (HA-buh-tatz)
Places where animals or plants normally live. A habitat may be the ocean, a jungle, a mountain, or a forest.

nutrients (NOO-tree-ents)
Substances needed by an animal or plant to help it grow and stay healthy.

origami (or-uh-GAH-mee)
The art of folding paper to make small models. Origami has been popular in Japan for hundreds of years. It gets its name from the Japanese words *ori*, which means "folding," and *kami*, which means "paper."

predators (PREH-duh-turz)
Animals that hunt and kill other animals for food.

prey (PRAY)
An animal that is hunted by another animal as food.

rain forests (RAYN FOR-ests)
Wooded habitats, which are often very warm, with a lot of rainfall and many types of animals and plants.

scavengers (SKAV-enj-urz)
Animals that usually eat the carcasses of dead animals. Some types of scavengers eat animal waste or dead plants.

wilderness (WIL-dur-nis)
A place where no humans live, such as a forest or desert.

territory (TER-uh-tor-ee)
The area where an animal lives, finds its food, and finds partners for mating.

For web resources related to the subject of this book, go to:
www.windmillbooks.com/weblinks
and select this book's title.

Read More

Clark, Willow. *Pandas*. The Animals of Asia. New York: PowerKids Press, 2012

de Lambilly-Bresson, Elisabeth. *Animals of the Mountains*. Animal Show and Tell. New York: Gareth Stevens Publishing, 2008.

Magby, Meryl. *Mountain Goats*. American Animals. New York: PowerKids Press, 2014.

Index